THE
RORSCHACH
GOD

STUDY GUIDE

Copyright © 2024 by Matthew Hester

Published by Unorthodox Resources

All rights reserved. No portion of this book may be reproduced, stored in a retrieval system, or transmitted in any form or by any means—electronic, mechanical, photocopy, recording, scanning, or other—except for brief quotations in critical reviews or articles, without prior written permission of the author.

All Scripture quotations are taken from The ESV® Bible (The Holy Bible, English Standard Version®), copyright © 2001 by Crossway, a publishing ministry of Good News Publishers. Used by permission. All rights reserved.

For foreign and subsidiary rights, contact the author.

Cover design by Sara Young
Cover photo by Andrew van Tilborgh

ISBN: 978-1-962401-76-0   1 2 3 4 5 6 7 8 9 10

Printed in the United States of America

THE
RORSCHACH
GOD

STUDY GUIDE

CONTENTS

CHAPTER 1. Shadows of the Divine 6

CHAPTER 2. God Stayed Silent 12

CHAPTER 3. The Role of Scripture 18

CHAPTER 4. Whatever Happened to the Trinity? 24

CHAPTER 5. Sermon on the Mount:
The Jesus (Godhead) Way 30

CHAPTER 6. What About the Violent God? 36

CHAPTER 7. What About the God Who
Craves Sacrifice? 42

CHAPTER 8. What Is God's Ideal? 48

CHAPTER 9. The Enemy's Table 54

CHAPTER 10. The Father Is Life, Light, and Love 60

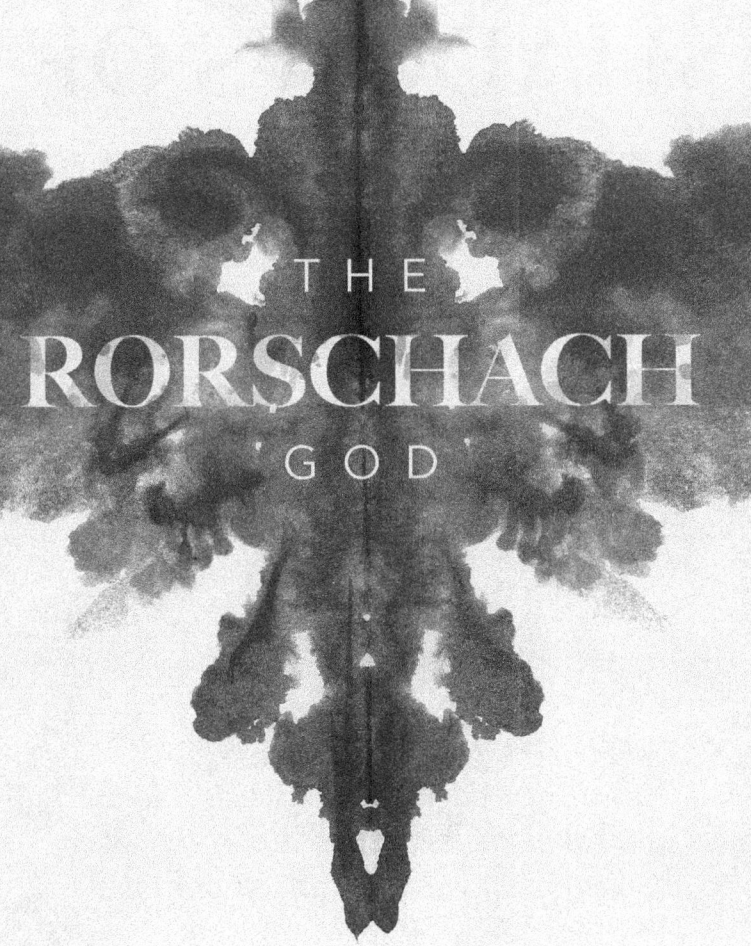

CHAPTER 1

SHADOWS OF THE DIVINE

Jesus is the bridge that helps us get to the heart of God's love and grace, going way beyond what we can grasp on our own.

READING TIME

As you read Chapter 1: "Shadows of the Divine" in The Rorschach God, *reflect on, and respond to the text by answering the following questions.*

REFLECT AND TAKE ACTION:

How does this chapter describe the common perception of God as both benevolent and indifferent, and what biblical examples can be used to illustrate this?

_____
_____
_____
_____
_____
_____
_____
_____
_____

Explain the significance of Jesus being described as the "perfect reflection of God" in the chapter. How does this align with biblical teachings?

_____
_____
_____
_____
_____
_____
_____
_____
_____

> *These are a shadow of the things to come,
> but the substance belongs to Christ.*
>
> **—Colossians 2:17**

Consider the scripture above and answer the following questions:

What is the meaning of this verse in your own words? What is it communicating about Christ?

_____

_____

_____

_____

_____

_____

_____

According to this chapter, why is it essential to understand God through the person of Jesus? Use the scriptural references provided within this chapter to support your answer.

_____

_____

_____

_____

_____

_____

_____

How does 1 John 3:2-3 contribute to the chapter's argument about the nature of God and the process of becoming like Christ?

What role do expectations and heart alignment play in perceiving the truth about God?

How does the chapter interpret John 14:9 and its significance in understanding the nature of God?

_____
_____
_____
_____
_____
_____
_____
_____
_____
_____

Discuss the contrast between Old Testament justice and the justice taught by Jesus.

_____
_____
_____
_____
_____
_____
_____
_____
_____
_____

What is the importance of seeing Jesus as the "exact representation of God's being" as stated in Hebrews 1:1-3, and how does this shape our understanding of God?

_____
_____
_____
_____
_____
_____
_____
_____
_____

How does the metaphor of Jesus as a bridge help explain God's love and grace?

_____
_____
_____
_____
_____
_____
_____
_____
_____

CHAPTER 2

GOD STAYED SILENT

The human propensity to mold God in their own flawed image often led to distorted representations.

READING TIME

As you read Chapter 2: "God Stayed Silent" in *The Rorschach God*, reflect on, and respond to the text by answering the following questions.

REFLECT AND TAKE ACTION:

What does Psalm 50:21 suggest about God's reaction to human behavior?

_____
_____
_____
_____
_____
_____
_____

How do the Psalms reflect the spiritual state of their writers?

_____
_____
_____
_____
_____
_____
_____

Why is it important to study the somber tones and themes in the Psalms?

_____
_____
_____
_____
_____
_____
_____

> *Abraham said, "God will provide for himself the lamb for a burnt offering, my son." So they went both of them together.*
>
> —**Genesis 22:8**

Consider the scripture above and answer the following questions:

What does this verse reveal about Abraham's faith in God?

_____
_____
_____
_____
_____
_____
_____
_____

In Psalm 50, what human behaviors does God criticize from verse 17 onward?

_____
_____
_____
_____
_____
_____
_____
_____

Why do you think people often reshape God in their own image?

___

What significant shift in humanity's perception of God occurred in Exodus 19?

___

How does the story of Abraham and Isaac reveal God's true character? What character does it reveal?

_____
_____
_____
_____
_____
_____
_____
_____

How does the narrative of Noah's flood challenge our understanding of God's nature?

_____
_____
_____
_____
_____
_____
_____
_____

What was Moses and Aaron's perception of God in their interactions with Pharaoh, and why is it significant?

_____
_____
_____
_____
_____
_____
_____
_____
_____

How does the crucifixion of Jesus serve as a paradox to many of the Old Testament depictions of God we once believed? Explain your answer.

_____
_____
_____
_____
_____
_____
_____
_____

CHAPTER 3

THE ROLE OF SCRIPTURE

The value of the Bible lies in its role as God's word, faithfully directing us to the living Word of God, Jesus Christ.

READING TIME

As you read Chapter 3: "The Role of Scripture" in *The Rorschach God*, reflect on, and respond to the text by answering the following questions.

REFLECT AND TAKE ACTION:

How does Robert Brinsmead's perspective differentiate between the Bible and the Word of God according to John 1:1?

_____
_____
_____
_____
_____
_____
_____
_____
_____
_____
_____

What is the primary purpose of Scripture as suggested in the chapter?

_____
_____
_____
_____
_____
_____
_____
_____
_____
_____
_____

> *Not that we are sufficient in ourselves to claim anything as coming from us, but our sufficiency is from God, who has made us sufficient to be ministers of a new covenant, not of the letter but of the Spirit. For the letter kills, but the Spirit gives life.*
>
> **—2 Corinthians 3:5-6**

Consider the scripture above and answer the following questions:

What is Paul communicating to the church of Corinth in this passage?

_____
_____
_____
_____
_____
_____
_____
_____

What is the contrast between the letters of the law and the Spirit?

How does biblical inerrancy potentially impose unrealistic expectations on Scripture?

_____
_____
_____
_____
_____
_____
_____
_____

What are some factual discrepancies within the Bible mentioned in the chapter, and how do they challenge the concept of inerrancy?

_____
_____
_____
_____
_____
_____
_____
_____

What criteria or perspectives might one use to discern the authority and relevance of different scriptures?

How does this chapter suggest understanding the inspiration of Scripture in light of the crucifixion of Jesus?

CHAPTER 4

WHATEVER HAPPENED TO THE TRINITY?

The Trinity asserts that at the core of God's eternal existence lies fellowship, other-centeredness, and approachability—the essence of communion characterized by self-giving and sacrifice in relationship to the other.

READING TIME

As you read Chapter 4: "Whatever Happened to the Trinity?" in *The Rorschach God*, reflect on, and respond to the text by answering the following questions.

REFLECT AND TAKE ACTION:

Explain the significance of Jesus Christ being described as "Father's eternal Son," "the One anointed in the Holy Spirit," and "the Creator and Sustainer of all things." How does this relate to the concept of the Trinity?

_____
_____
_____
_____
_____
_____
_____
_____
_____
_____

What is *perichoresis*, and how did the early church fathers use this concept to understand the Trinity?

_____
_____
_____
_____
_____
_____
_____
_____

How does the doctrine of the Trinity emphasize the importance of relationship, goodness, and love in the nature of God?

> "Yet a little while and the world will see me no more, but you will see me. Because I live, you also will live. In that day you will know that I am in my Father, and you in me, and I in you."
>
> —John 14:19-20

Consider the scripture above and answer the following questions:

What is Jesus speaking of in this passage?

How does the relationship between the Father, Son, and Holy Spirit establish a foundation of trust and love that extends to humanity?

_____
_____
_____
_____
_____
_____
_____
_____
_____
_____
_____
_____
_____

Discuss the role of the incarnation in revealing the relational nature of the Trinity. How do Jesus's divinity and humanity contribute to this understanding?

_____
_____
_____
_____
_____
_____
_____
_____

Analyze the significance of the incarnation as the coming of the eternal Trinitarian relationship into the world. How does this idea impact the understanding of God's interaction with humanity?

_____
_____
_____
_____
_____
_____
_____
_____

How do the New Testament passages, such as Colossians 1:19, 2:9, and John 1:14, reinforce the concept of the Trinity and the incarnation?

_____

_____

_____

_____

_____

_____

_____

_____

_____

How does this chapter suggest we should reinterpret Old Testament depictions of God that seem inconsistent with the nature of Jesus and the relational understanding of the Trinity?

_____

_____

_____

_____

_____

_____

_____

_____

_____

CHAPTER 5

SERMON ON THE MOUNT: THE JESUS (GODHEAD) WAY

We are called to submit the authority of our lives to Christ, allowing His goodness and love to flow through us.

READING TIME

As you read Chapter 5: "Sermon on the Mount: The Jesus (Godhead) Way" in *The Rorschach God*, reflect on, and respond to the text by answering the following questions.

REFLECT AND TAKE ACTION:

What is the central theme of Jesus's Sermon on the Mount, and how does it differ from the religious practices of His time?

_____
_____
_____
_____
_____
_____
_____
_____
_____

Discuss the significance of Jesus's statement, "I have not come to abolish the Law or the Prophets; I have come to fulfill them." How does this reshape traditional views of God's law?

_____
_____
_____
_____
_____
_____
_____
_____
_____

Explain how Jesus challenges the concept of retaliation ("an eye for an eye") in His teachings. What alternative does He propose, and why is this significant?

_____
_____
_____
_____
_____
_____
_____
_____
_____

> *"Do not think that I have come to abolish the Law or the Prophets; I have not come to abolish them but to fulfill them."*
> **—Matthew 5:17**

Consider the scripture above and answer the following questions:

Why is this verse significant?

_____
_____
_____
_____
_____
_____
_____

What does it mean for Jesus to "fulfill" the law and the prophets?

_____
_____
_____
_____
_____
_____
_____

What does Jesus reveal about God's character through His teachings on loving one's enemies? How does this contrast with traditional views of divine justice?

_____
_____
_____
_____
_____
_____
_____
_____

How does Jesus's teaching on mercy in the Beatitudes reflect the nature of the Godhead? Provide examples from Scripture to support your answer.

_____
_____
_____
_____
_____
_____

Discuss the concept of meekness as presented in the Sermon on the Mount. How does Jesus redefine strength in this context?

_____
_____
_____
_____
_____
_____

Explain the significance of the Beatitudes in understanding the kingdom of God. How do they challenge conventional ideas of righteousness and blessing?

_____
_____

In what ways does Jesus emphasize the importance of purity of heart? How does this relate to perceiving God and living a righteous life?

Compare and contrast Jesus's teachings on righteousness with the Old Testament laws. How does Jesus expand upon and fulfill these laws in His ministry?

CHAPTER 6

WHAT ABOUT THE VIOLENT GOD?

*The Lion conquers as the crucified Lamb.
This is who God has always been.*

READING TIME

As you read Chapter 6: "What About the Violent God?" in The Rorschach God, reflect on, and respond to the text by answering the following questions.

REFLECT AND TAKE ACTION:

Describe some of the violent images and actions attributed to God in the Old Testament. How do these portrayals challenge God's nature as is revealed through Jesus?

_____
_____
_____
_____
_____
_____
_____
_____
_____

Discuss the concept of the "Jesus Hermeneutic" as presented in this chapter. How does this approach help interpret the Old Testament's violent depictions of God?

_____
_____
_____
_____
_____
_____
_____
_____
_____

> *And one of the elders said to me, "Weep no more; behold, the Lion of the tribe of Judah, the Root of David, has conquered, so that he can open the scroll and its seven seals." And between the throne and the four living creatures and among the elders I saw a Lamb standing, as though it had been slain.*
>
> **—Revelation 5:5-6**

Consider the scripture above and answer the following questions:

Elaborate on the imagery in this passage. What is its significance to your understanding of Jesus Christ?

_____
_____
_____
_____
_____
_____
_____

In the context of Samuel's actions towards King Agag (1 Samuel 15), how does this chapter explore the portrayal of violence attributed to God through human agency? What conclusions can be drawn from this narrative?

_____
_____
_____
_____
_____
_____
_____

Explain the significance of Jeremiah's prophetic messages. How do these messages contribute to the discussion on violence and God's nature in the Old Testament?

_____
_____
_____
_____
_____
_____
_____
_____
_____
_____
_____
_____

What does this chapter suggest about the impact of violence, both prophetic and historical, on the characters such as Saul and David? How does this relate to their leadership and spiritual influence?

_____
_____
_____
_____
_____
_____
_____
_____

What lessons can be learned from Jesus's interactions with violence, as seen in the healing of Malchus's ear and His conversation with Pilate? How do these events contrast with conventional views of divine power and authority?

_____
_____
_____
_____
_____
_____
_____
_____

Discuss the symbolic imagery of Jesus as both the Lion of Judah and the Lamb of God. How does this dual imagery contribute to understanding His character and mission?

_____
_____
_____
_____
_____
_____
_____
_____
_____

How can Christians today apply the principles of nonviolence and the "Jesus Hermeneutic" when interpreting and responding to challenging passages about God's actions in the Bible?

_____
_____
_____
_____
_____
_____
_____
_____
_____

CHAPTER 7

WHAT ABOUT THE GOD WHO CRAVES SACRIFICE?

*Outside of relationship, God takes
no pleasure in what we offer.*

READING TIME

As you read Chapter 7: "What About the God Who Craves Sacrifice?" in *The Rorschach God*, reflect on, and respond to the text by answering the following questions.

REFLECT AND TAKE ACTION:

According to this chapter, what significant shift did Abraham experience regarding God's view of sacrifice? How do you think this impacted his understanding of God?

_____
_____
_____
_____
_____
_____
_____
_____
_____

How may the Egyptian sacrificial practices have influenced the Israelites, and what role did this influence play in Israel's adoption of sacrificial rituals?

_____
_____
_____
_____
_____
_____
_____
_____

In what ways does this chapter illustrate God's distinction from pagan gods? Provide specific examples discussed.

___

> "I hate, I despise your feasts,
> and I take no delight in your solemn assemblies.
> Even though you offer me your burnt offerings and grain offerings,
> I will not accept them;
> and the peace offerings of your fattened animals,
> I will not look upon them.
> Take away from me the noise of your songs;
> to the melody of your harps I will not listen."
>
> —Amos 5:21-23

Consider the scripture above and answer the following questions:

What is God communicating through Amos in these verses?

___

Describe King David's experience with sacrifice in 2 Samuel 24 and Psalm 51. How did these experiences challenge traditional views on sacrificial offerings?

_____
_____
_____
_____
_____
_____
_____

According to Psalm 50 and other passages, what does God truly desire from His people instead of sacrificial offerings?

_____
_____
_____
_____
_____
_____
_____

Discuss the prophetic critique of sacrificial practices in the Old Testament, as seen through the writings of Isaiah, Amos, and Jeremiah. What was God's message regarding these practices?

_____
_____
_____
_____
_____
_____
_____
_____

What did Jesus teach about sacrificial offerings, as mentioned in Matthew 22, Mark 12, and Hebrews 10? How did His teachings challenge traditional Jewish views on sacrifice?

_____
_____
_____
_____
_____
_____
_____
_____

How does the concept of Jesus as the self-sacrificial Lamb redefine the traditional understanding of sacrifice?

_____
_____
_____
_____
_____
_____
_____
_____
_____
_____

In what ways did the crucifixion of Jesus challenge and redefine the human perception of sacrifice? How does this event reflect God's true nature, as discussed in the chapter?

_____
_____
_____
_____
_____
_____
_____
_____
_____
_____

CHAPTER 8

WHAT IS GOD'S IDEAL?

Because God's love for people cannot be a control mechanism, He gently works alongside and within our flawed understanding of him, using His love to guide us toward a more Christlike expression of His ideals.

READING TIME

As you read Chapter 8: "What Is God's Ideal?" in *The Rorschach God*, reflect on, and respond to the text by answering the following questions.

REFLECT AND TAKE ACTION:

According to this chapter, what are the two main overarching themes of much of the Old Testament that God challenges directly?

_____
_____
_____
_____
_____
_____
_____
_____
_____
_____

Why can't God's love be a control mechanism?

_____
_____
_____
_____
_____
_____
_____
_____
_____

> *So we have come to know and to believe the love that God has for us. God is love, and whoever abides in love abides in God, and God abides in him.*
>
> —1 John 4:16

Consider the scripture above and answer the following questions:

What does this verse reveal about God's nature and God's ideal?

_____
_____
_____
_____
_____
_____
_____
_____
_____

What is God's ideal for marriage? Explain.

_____
_____
_____
_____
_____
_____
_____
_____
_____
_____
_____
_____
_____
_____
_____
_____
_____

Why did the nation of Israel desire a king?

_____
_____
_____
_____
_____
_____
_____
_____

What was God's original desire regarding kingship for Israel, and how did this differ from the surrounding nations?

_____
_____
_____
_____
_____
_____
_____
_____

What does Paul teach about warfare and Christian's response to violence?

_____
_____
_____
_____
_____
_____
_____
_____
_____
_____

Explain violent events of the Old Testament, like the conquest of Jericho, in light of God's character as revealed through Jesus.

_____
_____
_____
_____
_____
_____
_____
_____
_____
_____

CHAPTER 9

THE ENEMY'S TABLE

When we realize that Christ alone is our peace, we are then truly able to walk in peace with one another.

READING TIME

As you read Chapter 9: "The Enemy's Table" in The Rorschach God, reflect on, and respond to the text by answering the following questions.

REFLECT AND TAKE ACTION:

In what ways does Jesus's teaching on loving enemies challenge conventional views of justice and retribution?

_____
_____
_____
_____
_____
_____
_____
_____
_____
_____

How does Saul's encounter on the road to Damascus exemplify the unexpected ways God confronts and transforms those considered enemies?

_____
_____
_____
_____
_____
_____
_____
_____

How does this chapter interpret Jesus's actions towards Judas during the Last Supper, and what does this signify about God's response to human sinfulness?

_____
_____
_____
_____
_____
_____
_____
_____

> *You prepare a table before me in the presence of my enemies;*
> *you anoint my head with oil; my cup overflows.*
>
> **—Psalm 23:5**

Consider the scripture above and answer the following questions:

In your own words, what is the meaning of this psalm by David?

_____
_____

How does the cross illustrate God's radical approach towards those who oppose Him, and what implications does this hold for believers?

What ultimate enemy does Christ confront and overcome, and how does this victory redefine the concept of enmity in the context of faith?

_____
_____
_____
_____
_____
_____
_____
_____
_____
_____
_____
_____

How does the principle of loving one's enemies, as taught by Jesus, challenge traditional notions of justice and righteousness, and how should it shape our interactions today?

_____
_____
_____
_____
_____
_____
_____
_____
_____
_____
_____
_____

CHAPTER 10

THE FATHER IS LIFE, LIGHT, AND LOVE

He is flawless in every aspect: an overflowing wellspring of goodness.

READING TIME

As you read Chapter 10: "The Father Is Life, Light, and Love" in *The Rorschach God*, reflect on, and respond to the text by answering the following questions.

REFLECT AND TAKE ACTION:

In what ways is God the ultimate source and sustainer of life, and what implications does this have for our understanding of His nature?

_____
_____
_____
_____
_____
_____
_____
_____
_____
_____

Discuss the significance of God being described as light in 1 John. How does this attribute contrast with darkness and what does it reveal about God's character?

_____
_____
_____
_____
_____
_____
_____
_____
_____
_____

According to 1 John, how does God's love manifest in His willingness to send His Son as an atoning sacrifice for humanity?

_____
_____
_____
_____
_____
_____
_____

> "This is my commandment, that you love one another as I have loved you. Greater love has no one than this, that someone lay down his life for his friends."
>
> —John 15:12-13

Consider the scripture above and answer the following questions:

What stands out to you about this verse?

_____
_____
_____
_____
_____
_____
_____

What does this verse reveal about God's nature?

_____
_____
_____
_____
_____
_____
_____
_____
_____
_____
_____
_____
_____
_____

How does God's love restore and renew individuals and communities? Have you witnessed this in your own life or the lives of those around you?

_____
_____
_____
_____
_____
_____
_____
_____

Reflect on the idea that God's justice is restorative rather than punitive. How does this understanding challenge traditional views of justice and punishment?

_____
_____
_____
_____
_____
_____
_____
_____

Explore the relationship between God's love and discipline as discussed in this chapter. How does discipline differ from punishment in the context of God's parental care?

How does the revelation of God through Jesus Christ challenge our perceptions of God's wrath and justice?

www.ingramcontent.com/pod-product-compliance
Lightning Source LLC
Chambersburg PA
CBHW062122080426
42734CB00012B/2953